"Angel in My Lens"

Capturing God's Divine Beauty

Diane DiBlasi

4/23/2014

TABLE OF CONTENTS

Dedicated first and foremost to God, for without him we would have nothing, be nothing. Also to all souls in spirit and those still here in the physical, the Archangels, Ascended Masters, the prophets, teachers, and seers whom have come before us and have left their mark on this world and those whom we learn from each and every day as we continue on this journey we call life.

As I awaken each morning I start my day with gratitude and set my intentions for inner peace.

I thank God for the new dawn.

I ask for his Divine light to be with me as I go through my day.

I ask the four Archangels of the gates of heaven, Uriel, Gabriel, Raphael and Michael to protect me and protect all that I love.

My intentions I say every day.

I will not anger today.

I will not worry or fear today.

I will respect my teachers, parents and elders today.

I will work hard and honestly to make Earth as it is in Heaven today.

I will show love and kindness to all beings today.

I will not take anything personally today.

I will not make judgments or assumptions today.

I will be impeccable with my word today.

I will do my very best today.

I have created this book with the intention to share the beauty of God's world. I hope you will find inner peace as you go through these photos, and realize that all you have to do for inner peace is appreciate all of God's creations. Every day when you walk out of your home take notice of the sky, the colors of the trees, listen for which birds are close by singing their song. When you go for your walk or run, notice the flowers, feel the wind and know that God is nearby, for he never leaves us. For when you take notice of these little things in life you are thanking God for them all; you will then learn to find the peace within just by listening, seeing and appreciating. God so loved us all; that he has created this most wonderful world for us to enjoy. When we appreciate nature; that appreciation is passed on to our children and they grow with the understanding of what an exquisite world we live in; which is a gift to us all from our Creator.

"When we truly see and are grateful for all of God's Divine creations; we shall all know true inner peace that is within our souls" Diane DiBlasi

Acknowledgement

I give thanks to God, the Archangels, the Angels, my loved ones in spirit and of course my Kiana. Kiana I love you so and I know that you are with us each and every day as we go on this journey called "LIFE". You changed my life the day you were born and then again the day you crossed over to the light. You taught me much when you were here in the physical and even more now that you are in spirit. Your life and death has made me the person I am today and for that I am forever grateful... Mom.

♥ Love you for an eternity with all my heart and soul ♥

A Heartfelt thanks for all of my sisters and brothers, those of blood relation and those of the soul. There is a reason why each and every person comes in to one's life, weather for a reason, a season or a lifetime. There are lessons we all need to learn in life in order to prepare our souls for our destiny.

I would like to share with you a little about Kiana; this photo is one of my favorites. God blessed me with 3 beautiful daughters. Kiana is my eldest. She had strawberry blonde hair and the most unique eyes; they were different kind of brown with an orange tone. Her smile always lit up a room. Her sense of humor was amazing, she would always make you laugh and oh boy could she talk. Kiana had been living in Pennsylvania but we spoke on the phone every day. In 2009 Kiana passed away in her sleep, for that I am very grateful that she did not suffer; too many parents watch their children suffer prior to crossing over. We buried Kiana on the birthday of my youngest daughter and four days later this same daughter got married. So within a weeks' time I buried my eldest daughter and watched my youngest begin a new chapter in her life. The day of the wedding was such beautiful sunny day that we all knew that Kiana was there with us in spirit. It has taken some time for me to realize, but I can honestly tell you that Kiana's passing has been such a blessing to me. It is better to know someone's passing as a blessing rather than a loss; for if you grieve too deeply it can hold your loved one's soul back from evolving. There are two things that I keep in mind, I will feel my grief but not wallow in it and I honor the love for my daughter more than the loss. Kiana has such a strong spirit; I know that she is able to help many more people in spirit than she would have been able to in the physical. I also know that had she not crossed over I would not be on the spiritual path that I am on today. I thank her, the Angels and God every day for all the gifts and signs they send. Blessings to all whom come across this book (and those who do not), I pray you enjoy these photos in as much as I have enjoyed capturing each and every one of them. Namaste

"Autumn Colors"

Connetquot River State Park, Oakdale, NY

"God shows us the beauty of this wonderful season; sparkling colors of autumn how magnificent you are" Diane DiBlasi

I captured this particular photo on October 11, 2008. I remember the date because it was the 40th Angelversary (Anniversary) of my father's passing. We all know that there are no coincidences in life, the synchronicities that happen to us all has occurred just as planned. Even if we do not know why, we can be sure that our creator does. I was standing on a small wooden bridge over the Connetquot River taking photos of the flowing water. I turned around and I saw this beautiful tree with the sunlight shining through the water. When I was taking the first picture of this tree, I saw beautiful little sparkles of light in very vivid colors through the view finder, (Yes, I still use the view finder). I know that the spirits (God, my loved ones, the Angels,) were guiding me to take this photo. It was after taking this photo that I realized that I wanted to share my photos with the world; or at that time at least a few local galleries. This is the first photograph I ever matted and framed.

"Singing Yellow Warbler"

West Meadow Beach, East Setauket, NY

"How wondrous is the song of the sweet singing birds; they share with us all the beauty of their melodies" Diane DiBlasi

I captured the photo of this sweet little bird while walking on a mile long walkway that runs parallel to the shore line at the beach, on May 31, 2009. When strolling along this path you will encounter others whom enjoy jogging, running, biking, skate boarding and roller blading no matter what the season. Well, I remember that on this particular day it was quite warm outside, and I had decided to take a stroll near the beach. Although I was merely there for a stroll I had my camera with me, I always carry my camera for you never know what you might encounter. I was walking back to my car when I suddenly see a little yellow bird flying quite low across the road to the other side; he actually flew right in front of my face. I turned to see where he went and noticed he had landed on a bush and immediately started singing. What a blessing from God and the Angels to hear him sing and to be able to capture him while doing so. Just look at him, you can see the joy he is sharing with all of us.

"Mom's Love Rose"

"It's no wonder that the rose is synonymous with love; for when you look at it in full bloom and see its spiral, you can imagine it goes on for an eternity, just like love is never ending" Diane DiBlasi

I dedicate this photo to all moms everywhere, those in spirit and those still in the physical, also to all those who are living the role of a mom. I took this picture on August 19, 2009 in the office that I used to work at. My co-worker's mom sent her a bouquet of flowers for no particular reason, "just because" This act of love between mother and daughter and seeing these beautiful flowers touched my heart and soul. There was a variety of flowers in this bouquet; however this particular rose stood out among all the other flowers and I knew I had to capture its beauty and the love it represented forever.

"Monarch Beauty"

Dahlia Garden, Bayard Arboretum State Park, Great River, NY

"The Monarch is the loving butterfly that goes from flower to flower and as it does, it touches many souls sharing its beauty with us all"

Diane DiBlasi

"Wings of a Monarch"

A Butterfly, who doesn't like butterflies, I would think most people do. Of all the insects in the world I would think that the butterfly has the most spiritual meaning to most people. It is a symbol of transformation, like the butterfly whose life changes from one extreme to another, so can an individual change many times in their life. I took these two photos on October 4, 2008, this little Monarch was making his way around from flower to flower and yes, and both pictures feature the same butterfly. I know since my daughters passing she has sent me many signs in the form of a butterfly. These pictures were actually taken a year prior to her passing; perhaps this little guy was a sign from another loved one in heaven. For our loved ones never really leave us, they have just returned to their true state of being. Remember we are souls having a human experience.

"Follow Me"

Pine Lake, Coram, NY

"Learning, living and growing will always lead you home, no matter where you go" Diane DiBlasi

On April 23, 2009 I took this picture of this juvenile Mute Swan residing at a small lake near my hometown. I had been taking photos of this particular swan and its parents for a few weeks. The day I took this picture, the father swan was chasing this juvenile around the lake until it left the main lake and went into a small run off of the lake that had occurred from a lot of rain earlier in the month. I thought it was odd that the father would not let his offspring stay in the lake with him and his mate. Well I found out later that day that fledglings usually remain close to their parents for continued protection and brooding until the next spring. Upon learning this, the scene I witnessed between father and son became quite clear. A few weeks later I returned to the lake to discover that the juvenile had finally found the courage to venture off on its own. I do have such a fascination with these swans, which is another story for another day, another page.

"Mesmerized Frog"

Back Yard Pond

"It's all in the timing; patience and divine timing will lead you to where you need to be" Diane DiBlasi

We had a little pond in our back yard that I had put in myself. I loved watching the fish swim, grow and have babies. Sometimes I would discover a new resident in the pond, like a turtle or a frog, this little frog was one of those new residents. I loved when I would catch a glimpse of this little guy for whenever he heard or saw anyone coming in the back yard he would immediately jump back into the water; I guess he was a little camera shy. I used to try to sneak up very quietly to be able to watch him; so you can imagine how thrilled I was on this particular day, June 5, 2008, when he sat there and allowed me to photograph him. The sun was just at the right angle in the sky that you can see the brightness in his eyes. When you are patient and positive, know that what you wish to achieve will happen all in divine timing, after all it is the law of attraction.

"Morning Angel Light"

Lloyd Harbor, NY

"Be grateful for each new dawn…for it may be your last as you know it. Life brings changes, embraces these changes and you embrace God"

Diane DiBlasi

I took this picture in the very early morning of August 16, 2008; I was driving down a road on my way to Caumsett State Park in Lloyd Harbor, NY to capture more nature photos. The road was a very dark tree lined street and I was the only car on the road. I was coming around this bend in the road and suddenly there was a light coming through the trees, the brightness actually blinded me and I had to stop the car; of course I grabbed my camera and started taking pictures. I had matted this photo but have not shown it to anyone until I shared it on my Face book page on June 26, 2013. I was guided by my angels to post this photo for I thought it was appropriate to show my Love for a new day and of course God whom created it... "Embrace each day as if it were your last". Can you see the angel in this picture? Look not far from the left side of the double yellow line, and you will see the angel. I can assure you that no one was standing in the middle of the road when I took this photo. I am truly grateful for being in the right place at the right time; although I do believe that if the angels wish to appear to you it will happen no matter where you are. I so love God, the Archangels, and the angels with all my heart and soul.

"Doe in Summer Reeds"

Fire Island, NY

"See only love, gratitude and joy in each other and you will see and know how God wishes us to be" Diane DiBlasi

This picture is a favorite of many people who see my photos; I captured it when I went down to the beach on June 7, 2008 to take pictures of the Fire Island light house. If you choose not to walk along the shore line you can walk on the wooden walkways which have bushes and plants on either side. As I was walking back to my car I was taking pictures of the many different flowers that caught my eye. Well in the high reeds I saw this doe eating with her backside facing me. Naturally I didn't want just a picture of her backside, so I made some calling noises to get her attention and she turned her head around and looked directly at me as if to say "yes, can I help you?" I captured her just as she turned around and then I thanked her for allowing me to take her picture. One year I framed it for my uncle Al who was like a father to my siblings and I when we were children since our own father had passed when we were very young. Well I can tell you the gratitude and joy that I saw in his eyes the day I gave it to him; it has certainly imprinted upon my soul.

To all the Uncle AL's of the world, God Bless and rest in peace I know you all will, for you are all with the Angels in Heaven.

"Playful American Goldfinch"

Back Yard Willow Tree

"Of all the gifts God has bestowed on us, I believe the birds are the most curious and wondrous to watch" Diane DiBlasi

In the spring of 2010 my husband and I moved to a place little further out east then where we had lived previously. The grounds around my new home were like being in a park with lots of Pine and Weeping Willow trees. Well on August 21, 2010 I had my back door open and I heard the beautiful song of this little guy, naturally I grabbed my camera and went to see where the song was coming from. I saw in the Weeping Willow this playful little American Goldfinch. He was jumping around from branch to branch and from tree to tree. At one point I know he became just as curious about me as I was about him; he started to look directly at me and was even cocking his head to the side. This little guy brought joy to me while I was taking his pictures; I truly believe he really enjoyed having the attention and having his picture taken. When we notice and listen to the sounds of nature and enjoy them, we are giving thanks to God for all of the gifts he bestows upon us.

"Let's do this together"

Connetquot River State Park, Oakdale, NY

"When we give courage to each other; we can accomplish all that we set out to do" Diane DiBlasi

I took this picture on October 4, 2008, while I was standing on a bridge over the Connetquot River taking pictures of the fall foliage. I saw these two Canadian Geese swimming towards the bridge; I started taking some photos of them. As they approached, they stopped and looked at me; they seemed to hesitate to continue under the bridge. They turned around and started to go back the way they had come and then they seemed to change their mind and turned around again to swim towards the bridge. They then stopped and looked at each other as if they were giving each other courage to continue under the bridge, saying "we can do this, let's do this together." I just love the way they are looking at each other as they swam under the bridge side by side. Oh yeah, I also love the reflection of the fall foliage in the water.

"Rainbow Spirit"

"Spirit may be seen in many forms and send messages in many ways, just open your heart, eyes and soul to see and know the love they always bring"
Diane DiBlasi

I left the house very early in the morning to take pictures of the sunrise out east, well coming home this particular morning while driving on route 25 I saw many Blue Jays on the side of the road. Blue Jays have always been one of my favorite birds since I was a child; I knew I had to pull over to get some photos of them. Well, when I got out of the car they all flew away even though I tried to be very quiet. I decided to stay around to see if they came back. A few of them did and I focused on this particular Blue Jay in this photo and took quite a few pictures of him hopping from one branch to another.   When I got home and downloaded the photos on my computer I saw next to the Blue Jay in two of the pictures was a rainbow orb (rainbow spirit), the rainbow is almost transparent, you can see the bark of the tree through the rainbow, and in a vertical position, shaped like an oval quite larger than the bird. In one of the pictures he is clearly looking at this orb.   The date these were taken was Nov. 14, 2010. (I realized the date that I took these pictures about a year later) It turns out that it was a day before my company that I worked with for 14 years had let me go. I made a lot of mistakes, because within that last year my daughter Kiana passed in October 2009, a close uncle passed away in February 2010 and then my mother passed away in August 2010...three family members in 10 months. I believe spirit guided me out of that mundane job and I am forever grateful. Just recently an intuitive told me that this particular rainbow spirit is a part of a spirit realm that has not been written much about yet. If you have any information you would like to share or have questions regarding this particular spirit picture please feel free to email me at: kianasangels09@gmail.com

"Bird in Hand"

Elizabeth A. Morton Wildlife Refuge, Sag Harbor, NY

"When we connect with nature, we connect with ourselves and with God's wondrous gifts" Diane DiBlasi

To hold a small bird in your hand is truly a gift and a wonder. This particular picture was taken on December 30, 2008; it was extremely cold that day. If you like birds this wildlife refuge is a place to go to enjoy these little guys up close and personal. This little Black Capped Chickadee is sitting on my brother's hand; you see when you go to this refuge always bring some bird seed with you. With some bird seeds and a little patience you will experience something magical. The first time you feel these tiny little creatures on your hand you will be amazed at how light they are and you will want them to come help themselves to the seeds in your hand over and over again. Why not go to your local wildlife refuge, park or even your own back yard; bring some seeds and patience and wait for the magic to happen.

"Tufted Titmouse"

Elizabeth A. Morton Wildlife Refuge, Sag Harbor, NY

"The act of giving is like no other, for when you give from your heart and soul, you receive more than you expected" Diane DiBlasi

I took this photograph on August 17, 2008; I took my sister to the wildlife refuge I love so much. I always want to share this place with as many people as I can. When you go there you can always expect a Black Capped Chickadee to come swooping down from the trees to help itself to a seed or two from your hand. It is not too often that a Tufted Titmouse is willing to mingle with humans as readily as the Chickadees. My sister was quite surprised and pleased that he chose to sit on her hand to feed. I was very thrilled and grateful to capture this cute little guy. Be grateful for all things in life. For even the small things, such as touching a little bird is a testament of God's love for us all.

"Meg's Roses"

"To look at the beauty of a rose is to look at the unfolding of life's wonderful beginnings and the love in another's heart" Diane DiBlasi

This picture was taken on October 12, 2009, the day after my youngest daughter's wedding; they are from the centerpiece on one of the tables. My father had passed away on October 11, 1968 and when my daughter got engaged and was deciding when her wedding would be, she asked me if grandma would mind if she got married on this date. Well I asked mom if it would be fine if Megan got married on October 11th. Mom looked at me with a smile and said she "would not mind for it will make it a good day with good memories". Megan went on with the plans for the wedding. Meanwhile my oldest daughter Kiana lived in another state and was planning on coming to the wedding, well we all know sometimes God has different plans then we do. Late night on the 2nd of October my husband and I were getting ready for bed; we got a knock on the door and were very surprised when a police officer was standing on our front patio. My first thought was that something happened to my middle daughter for she was out with some friends and this was after all a local police officer. Well it turned out he came to tell us that my oldest daughter Kiana had passed away earlier that day. We had buried Kiana on my youngest daughter's birthday and four days later she had her wedding. Before the wake Megan did tell me that her and Dennis would postpone the wedding and I told her "not at all, a wedding is a new beginning and you should still go on with it, Kiana would want you to". (So in one weeks' time I buried my eldest and watched my youngest start a new chapter in life.) They say that God does not give you more than you can handle, I know that I was not fully mentally present at the wedding but I know for certain that my angel Kiana was there in spirit with us all. The next day I was sitting at the dining room table and the sun was shining through the windows just at the right angle and I took these three roses out of the centerpiece and laid them down on the table and snapped this picture. I love how the sunlight is shining down on them. Just as I am writing this, I realized that each one of these roses represents each one of my beautiful daughters and the love we have for each other. I am forever grateful that God has blessed and trusted me to be their mother.

"Winter Blue"

West Meadow Beach, East Setauket, NY

"Thank you God for the cold of winter days, for it refreshes the earth as well as the soul; and prepares us for new beginnings in spring" Diane DiBlasi

This photo was taken on December 13 2008; on this particular day the temperature was only around 18 degrees. The name of this photo does not indicate what some people make think of as "Winter Blues"; I chose this name because when you go to the beach or any body of water in the winter and take pictures, the colors are much more vivid than any other time of year. Looking at the blues in this photo, how crisp the colors are you just know it had to be very cold outside. The beach is beautiful anytime of the year; however in the winter it is just so serene and peaceful. Going to the beach in the winter is one of my favorite things to do; good thing I like the winter. God has made beauty in all the seasons; I thank God for them all and yes even the winter when it is bitter cold outside.

"Sunrise at Montauk Point"

Montauk, NY

"Sunrise, sunsets is the magical way of how nature begins and ends each day; view and rejoice each of these and know the love and peace of God's world that is in your heart and soul" Diane DiBlasi

Who doesn't like sunrises and sunsets. It is easier to catch a sunset than a sunrise for most people due to the early hour one has to wake in order to catch a sunrise. This photo was captured on March 7, 2009 about 70 miles from my home. I remember getting up very early, probably around 3 or 4 am to make the long drive out to the east end of Long Island. Here on the island you could see a bumper sticker on someone's car that just says "The End", being from the island you just know it means Montauk Point, which is the end on the south fork of Long Island. When I arrived at "The End" it was still dark outside, it was very peaceful to be on a beach with no one else there. I was standing on this hill, watching the sun come up over the horizon, and I realized there is just something magical about watching the dawn of a new day. Everyone should take the opportunity to watch a sunrise at least once in their lifetime; for it is just so exhilarating. What better way to thank God for the starting of a new day.

"Sunset Sail"

Cedar Beach, Mount Sinai, NY

"Sunsets mark the end of each day that God has granted us; the colors of the sunsets reflect God's magnificent palette for us to enjoy" Diane DiBlasi

This sunset was captured on July 9, 2009. As a nature photographer I am always amazed that when you capture sunsets from one day to the other; the uniqueness of the moment captured is as different as each day that follows. Sunsets come at the end of each day, and each one having its own unique feel. It is fitting that each sunset has its own blend of colors; you could have lots orange and peach one day and the next day have lots of purple, yellow and pink in the sunset. Sunsets do remind me of the beauty of each day that God has granted us. As each end of the day comes; God shows us thru the sun's setting the everlasting beauty of the world and for that we should be forever grateful.

"The Gift"

Shenandoah National Park, VA

"Notice the gifts that are given each day; be grateful for these gifts no matter how small and your heart will be open to all the love it can hold" Diane DiBlasi

This photo was captured on October 5, 2012. Each year since 2007, my sisters and I have gone to Shenandoah National Park to hike and spend time together, no husbands or children. You see I have a lot of sisters and we do enjoy each other's company. In 2012 we hiked a trail called Stony Man Trail; even though this hike is only 1.6 miles round trip, it is one of the most spectacular views on the mountain. It is the second highest peak in the park (4011 feet) and one of our favorites. This was not the first year we climbed Stony Man, however it is one we will never forget. Once we reached the top we stayed and took lots of pictures and then started to go back down the trail. At one point one sister noticed that a butterfly was in a tree, of course we all pulled out our cameras and started shooting. As you know butterflies do not settle very long for a photo shoot, however he did seem to stay for longer than normal. He then started to fly away; going down the mountain. Then he turned and flew back by us. We were so intrigued by this little being coming back to us that we just stood there. He then flew circles around our heads and proceeded to land on one sister's head then on another sister's head. I then instinctively told everyone "put your hands up in the air, he is going to land on someone's hand". Immediately we all did hold our arms straight up in the air; palms flat and he landed on my hand. It was just so exhilarating, we all got so excited, and we were like children again. I naturally started to cry, knowing this was a sign and gift from my daughter Kiana. As you can see I always put a name to each photo and one of my sisters' suggested the name of this photo should be

"The Gift"

"The Second Gift"

"Butterfly, oh sweet butterfly come visit with me when I am still, then I should know that your love is with me for an eternity" Diane DiBlasi

These two photos were captured on October 6, 2012. My sisters and I were hiking on a trail in Shenandoah National Park called Mill Prong Trail which is 2.7 miles round trip. This is a beautiful trail through the forest down to Rapidan Camp, which was President Hoover's weekend retreat. After hiking about .7 miles down which is where these photos were taken, you then reach a stream. My sister Donna and I were down by the stream waiting for my other sisters and I noticed this little butterfly sunning himself on the rocks at the river's edge. He didn't seem to mind or notice that we were taking pictures of him. I told my sister, "slowly put your hand down by the butterfly and he will crawl on your hand". I don't know how I knew he would, I just listened to my intuition, she did so and he did exactly what I knew he would. I have always had a close connection with nature, it seems fitting that I have chosen to be a nature photographer. One of my greatest joys is to share my photos with others whom love God's beautiful world.

"Angels, a Gift from God"

"God Sends His Love on Angel Wings"

Unknown Author

"In God's infinite wisdom, he created the angels for all of us" Diane DiBlasi

What we can do for our Creator:

In Happy moments, praise God.

In Difficult moments, seek God.

In Quiet moments, worship God.

In Painful moments, trust God.

And every moment, thank God.

Unknown author

We can thank God for all gifts including Angels and the Archangels. The word angel means "messenger." Angels bring messages from Our Divine Creator and our loved ones that are in spirit. Heaven and Earth are united with the help of God's Angels. When you work with the angels you are showing God gratitude for his gifts and in turn are closer to God.

Everyone has been told since they were a child that they have a Guardian Angel. This is true; however, has anyone ever told you that you have many Angels with you. You can and should ask for their help with anything. They are waiting to hear from you. What we all need to know and remember is that because of our free will as Human Beings they cannot help us with our daily lives or our needs and problems unless we ask them. When we invite angels into our lives each day, we evolve spiritually by reuniting Heaven and Earth within. The Archangels and Angels are waiting for you, they want to help us in every way they can. There is no task too small or large that they cannot help us with, try something small first, ask the angels; when you are about a mile away from the mall to please have a parking spot close to the door of one of the stores you are going to, I do this all the time and I always get the spot I need, even if it is in a tourist town in the summer. Remember, always good intentions and harm to none. Angels will help all beings spiritually as well as in practical ways. Once you start to communicate with the Archangels and Angels you will notice that your life will improve and you will have such inner peace.

I leave you for now, with one final photo…

"Peace of God"

South shore beach, Long Island, N.Y.

May you all know the peace of God's Love.

May you see all beings as a soul and a child of God.

May you have all of Gods Loving Angels with you each and every day.

Love you all with all of my heart and soul...

If you would like to see more of the photos I have taken please go to my website at:

www.hearingyourangels12.com

Please leave a comment about any of my photos or my book on the comment page.

I thank you for purchasing a copy of my book.

I pray that you have a wonderful blessed day.

I pray that you have all the peace and abundance from the universe, to stay with you all the days of your life.

God and Angel Blessings to you.

Diane DiBlasi

Made in United States
North Haven, CT
20 May 2023